First Edition
Genuine Autographed Collectible

Do you want me to sign it in ink or in lipstick?

Gift Card

Date:

To:

From:

Message

What Do Books Do?
BOOKS ARE POWERFUL
Books Educate!
Book Enlighten!
Books Empower!
Books Emancipate!
Books Entertain!
Books Spring Eternal!
Books Drive Exploration!
Books Spark Evolution!
Books Ignite Revolution!

Sharon Esther Lampert

Gift Shop: BooksArePowerful.com

Literature, Poetry, Self-Help, Relationships, Romance, Love, Marriage, Sex, Sharon Esther Lampert

Cupid: The Language of Love in Letter C

©2023 by Sharon Esther Lampert. All Rights Reserved.
No part of this book may be used or reproduced in any manner whatsoever without written permission except in the case of brief quotations embodied in critical articles and reviews.

KADIMAH PRESS
GIFTS OF GENIUS

Books may be purchased for education, business, or sales promotional use.

ISBN Hardcover: 978-1-885872-55-5
ISBN Paperback: 978-1-885872-56-2
ISBN E-Book: 978-1-885872-57-9
Library of Congress Catalog Card Number: 2022909645

Fan Mail:
www.SharonEstherLampert.com
FANS@SharonEstherLampert.com

For Global Online Orders and Distribution:
INGRAM 1 Ingram Blvd. La Vergne, TN 37086-3629
Phone: 615-793-5000, Fax orders: 615-287-6990
Global Bookstores: USA, CAN, UK, AUS, EU, ASIA, AFRICA

Book Design and Interior: Creatve Genius Sharon Esther Lampert
Editor: Dave Segal

First Edition

Manufactured in the United States of America

CUPID

The Language of Love in Letter C

KADIMAH PRESS
Gifts of Genius

"The **Sole** Intention of My Poetry
is to Add LIGHT to Your **Soul**"

"**Food** is for the **Body**
Education is for the **Mind**
Poetry is for the **Soul**"

"I AM an OPENBook, to
KNOWME is to README"

"Every Thought in Your Head
Was Put There by a Writer"

"When I'm not Writing
I'm Reading. When I'm not
Writing or **Reading**, I'm Singing."

"Please Don't Let Me Die with a Typo!"

For Clark, My Muse, Happy Birthday!

"It's not the men in my life that counts;
it's the life in my men!"
—Mae West

No **F**akes!
No **F**at!
No **F**luff!
No **F**iller!
No **F**lops!
No **F**-Bomb!

Also by The Pr**od**i**g**y

Sharon Esther Lampert's Mind Conceptualizes
BIG IDEAS
Using One Letter of the Alphabet

What Do Books Do?
—Written in Letter **E**

Seven Goalposts of Education for Lifelong Learners
—Written in Letter **E**

Sharon's Bio—Written in Letters **F, B** and **P**

Make Life Make **S**ense
TEMPORARY INSANITY
We Are All Building Our Lives on a **S**and Trap
—Written in Letter **S**

THE SECRET SAUCE OF BOOK SALES
How to Make Money Selling Books
—Written in Letter **P**

DESTINY
Are You Living Your Life By **D**efault or by **D**esign?
—Written in Letter **D**

WIN AT THIN
FAT ME! SKINNY ME!
What Works What Doesn't
—Written in Letter **A**

Table of Contents

1. Connection
2. Chemistry
3. Communication
4. Common Ground
5. Comfortable
6. Complexity
7. Compatibility: We Just Clicked!
8. Companionship & Courtship
9. Challenges: Change Him! Control Her!
10. Compromise
11. Collaboration or Competition?
12. Change Him!
13. Control Her!
14. Conflict: Counseling & Consensus
15. Conditional and Unconditional Love
16. Crisis! Curse! Closure!
17. Culture of Casual Sex
18. Currency: Charm & Charisma
19. Carefree
20. Commitment
21. Celebration
22. Consummation: Children or Creativity

How to Read a Poem By Sharon Esther Lampert
About the Prodigy
FAN MAIL
BOOKSTORE

Sharon Esther Lampert

Connection

Cupid: The Language of Love in Letter C

Step 1. Connection

On the last cold rainyday of winter,
lingering on into the month of May,
we meet in the middle of a street.
He knows my first name, but not my last
and we can't remember how we met.
Every creature on earth is meeting,
greeting, and preening. Mother nature
is the matchmaker, the yenta busybody
who has set the trap. I am cold, in need of a
sweater and a warm heart and hand to hold.
I am both vulnerable and vixen, a vessel
ready to be boarded by a seafaring sailor.

Sharon Esther Lampert

Chemistry

Cupid: The Language of Love in Letter C

Step 2. Chemistry

We stop and stare.
He is tall and handsome.
He is warm and inviting.
We have dinner at Tiny Thai.
I warm up on hot sake and Tom Kha Gai soup.
We celebrate his belated birthday.
We stop at Starbucks for decaffeinated tea,
and share a chocolate brownie and kisses.
His heart is open and his arms are strong.
Unlike Cinderella, at the stroke of midnight
I am lost in his embrace, drinking his sweet
elixir of kisses. Two hearts are set aflame.

Sharon Esther Lampert

Communication

Cupid: The Language of Love in Letter C

Step 3. Communication

We talk about this, that, and the other.
It is impossible to know another person.
How was your day? We take another trip
to Peruvian Pio Pio for a belated (May 9th)
Cinco de Mayo celebration (May 5th).
We have become world travelers.
At this juncture in time, I at least know
who I am. We celebrate his good fortune.
We explore Six Handles, the most popular
frozen yogurt joint of sweet confections.
We share dessert to maintain our figures.
He likes hard ice cream. His favorite is Rocky Road.
We are full but a hunger for love lingers.
We share a non-caloric kiss, and then another.
The world disappears into the background.
Neighbors feel the love emanating from our
embrace and shout out,"It's true love!"
His hand has taken hold of my magnificent breast.
The passion between us is spreading
like a raging wildfire, uncontainable.

Cupid: The Language of Love in Letter C

Step 4. Common Ground

We love learning new things.
He is signed up for a non-credit course.
My mind is a private university where
he can enroll and take a class.

Cupid: The Language of Love in Letter C

Step 5. Comfortable

He is like a plush teddy bear on the outside.
but on the interior insecurities are percolating.
Demons dance to defeat. He is still single,
in search of a sacred sanctuary built for two.
I am a special-needs child. My gifts are my glory.

Sharon Esther Lampert

Complexity

Cupid: The Language of Love in Letter C

Step 6. Complexity

Intimacy is a complex equation of compound variables: mind, body, and spirit.
You get everything you want and don't want in the same person!
Is he a prospect or a project? (project: He needs a full-time psychiatrist!)
Dating apps recommend, "Be the Chooser, not the Choice!"
LOVE IS BLIND! Why? Because you can never know another person!
You marry a stranger!
You have sex with a stranger!
You have children with a stranger!
You divorce a stranger!
I want to be a man's third wife:
- The first wife is a slave.
- The second wife is another failed attempt to get it right.
- By the third wife, he has given up, time is running out, and he wants to enjoy what time is left — **my perfect guy!**

Sharon Esther Lampert

Compatibility

Cupid: The Language of Love in Letter C

Step 7. Compatibility: We Just Clicked!

I am Leo the lioness. He is Taurus the bull.
We are both fixed organizers (stubborn).
I am positive masculine. I am the Sun.
He is negative feminine. He is Venus.
I am fire, adding **LIGHT**, making things grow.
He is earth: tactile, stable, sensual, and erotic.
I am a **QUEEN**. We are both the boss and bossy.
We are destined for a collision, a battle of
wills in the boardroom, not the bedroom.
Opposites don't attract, they attack!

Cupid: The Language of Love in Letter C

Step 8. Companionship & Courtship

Who is he?
A date, one-night stand, lover, friend,
playmate, boyfriend or husband?
Courtship: I enjoy dating, and having a playmate
who loves N.Y.C. nightlife: Broadway, ballet,
concerts, museums, sports, and travel.
Candlelight dinners are charming.
I propose: "Friends First & Forever!"
He says, "Yes!" I arrive bearing a gift!

Sharon Esther Lampert

Challenges

Cupid: The Language of Love in Letter C

Steps 9. Challenges: Change Him! Control Her!

Proceed with Caution: Character Flaws!

Capricious? Cheater? Cheap? Covetous? Control Freak? Corrupt? Cruel?

Does he have a conscience?

Are you conscious or unconscious?

Where is he? Confident? Courteous? Calm? Compassionate? Chivalrous?

Sharon Esther Lampert

Compromise

Cupid: The Language of Love in Letter C

Step 10. Compromise: I, You, We
3 LIVES is the formula for success: Mine, Yours, and Ours.

Cupid: The Language of Love in Letter C

Step 11. Collaboration or Competition?

Can we work together sharing responsibilities:
Chores: cooking, cleaning, car washes, raising a few cubs, emptying cat's litter box, and copulation and orgasms — or is everything a toxic-masculinity competition?
He complains: "That's women's work!"
Did you just call me a cunt behind my back?
"No, never cupcake! You are the sweet cream in my coffee!"

Sharon Esther Lampert

Change Him!

Cupid: The Language of Love in Letter C

Step 12. Change

Can he grow, ripen, and mature?
Or is he set in his ways, a dinosaur on the verge of extinction?

Sharon Esther Lampert

Cupid: The Language of Love in Letter C

Step 13. Control

Can we share control? Boss or bossy?
I need to be in control or I'm out of control!
Is he contentious and combative or courteous and considerate?
Is marriage a relic of a bygone era of subordination of women as servants and servitude? Emotional vulnerability takes courage!

Sharon Esther Lampert

Conflicts

Cupid: The Language of Love in Letter C

Step 14. Conflicts: Counseling & Consensus

Change Him! Control Her! Clash, Crash, and Crumble!
Let's set up a marriage-counseling appointment before it's too late!
Bring your suicase! How many suitcases? One suitcase for each decade of life!
I didn't cause it! I can't control it! I can't cure it!

Q. Do you compliment or complain and criticize? Are you contemptuous?
Q. Do you contribute or contaminate?
Q. Are you compassionate or cruel? Are you catfishing my online profile?
Q. Are you cheerful and calm or caustic and chaotic?
Q. Are you ready to come clean and confess your cheating double life?
Q. Let's talk about cunilingus! Where do you want to be caressed?
Q. Are you taking Cialis to augment your carnal cravings?
Q. Can we negotiate a fair resolution—and reach a consensus?

A Loveless Marriage is the Loneliest Place in the World!

Dealbreakers: Disrespect & Divorce — We treat each other like Disposables! Duh!

Conversation is an art & science: Be present, mirror, validate, and ask questions. Master these critical core competency communication tools to keep your intimate relationship on track for Happily Ever After!

Read My Book:
"LYMTY: Love You More Than Yesterday"
14 Relationship Strategies for **Happily After Ever!**

Step 15. Conditional and UnConditional Love

You Don't Find Love, You Create Love! Practice Understanding & Respect!

TRUE LOVE is unconditional love. Unconditional love is real — but rare!

The most important relationship is the one you have with yourself!
Self-Love is True Love! Love from outside yourself is Bonus Love!

Adult Love is Mostly Conditional Love:
- People don't love you — they love only what they want from you!
- People don't have enough love for self-love — let alone to love you!
- You can never know another person! It takes a lifetime to know yourself!
- For unconditional TRUE LOVE ... get a loyal pet!

"You Don't Find Love, You Create Love!"

— Philosopher Queen Sharon Esther Lampert

Sharon Esther Lampert

Crisis

Cupid: The Language of Love in Letter C

Step 16. Crisis! Curse! Closure!

The CURSE! 99.9% of personal relationships are love-hate relationships.
All people **help you** with their strengths & **hurt you** with their weaknesses.
A warm nobody is better than a cold somebody!
One chapter closes and other chapter opens.
Love me or leave me! CLOSURE!

All people help you with their strengths and hurt you with their weaknesses!

— Philosopher Queen Sharon Esther Lampert

A warm nobody is better than a cold somebody!

— Philosopher Queen Sharon Esther Lampert

Cupid: The Language of Love in Letter C

Step 17. Culture of Casual Sex

- Sex First, Love Maybe, Marriage Never!
- Hot Sex Forever — Married Sex No More!
- Single & Lonely, Married & Miserable or Divorced & Bitter
- Friends with Benefits!
- Marriage contracts till death-do-us-part are anachronistic.

SEX FIRST! LOVE MAYBE! MARRIAGE NEVER!
— Philosopher Queen Sharon Esther Lampert

HOT SEX FOREVER MARRIED SEX NO MORE!
— Philosopher Queen Sharon Esther Lampert

Single & Lonely Married and Miserable Divorced and Bitter
— Philosopher Queen Sharon Esther Lampert

Cupid: The Language of Love in Letter C

Step 18. Currency — Charm & Charisma

Since Tarzan and Jane — is biology destiny?
A woman's social currency is her youth, beauty, charm, and sexuality.
A man's social currency is his charisma, professional status, and financial success.
Men gain status by what they do — women gain status by who they're with.
Men offer security — but not fidelity — women offer fertility and family.
Women have more power in the bedroom — and in the world.
Women know where their clitoris is — and will no longer fake an orgasm to climax.
Are you cumming? Did you cum? I'm cumming now! Let's cozy up & cuddle!
Consent is the issue of the day. "No!" means "No!"
There are **14 GLOBAL CATASTROPHES** of violence against women #MeToo
Couple nicknames like Cutie pie and Cupcake never go out of fashion!

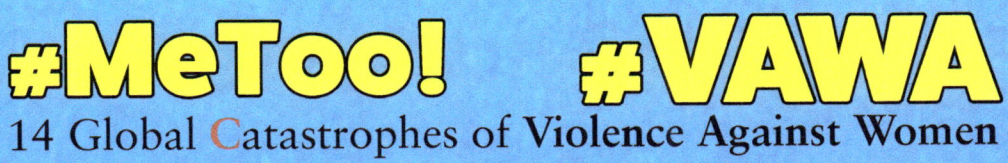

#MeToo!   #VAWA
14 Global Catastrophes of Violence Against Women
Read My Book: SILLY LITTLE BOYS.com

Sharon Esther Lampert

Carefree

Cupid: The Language of Love in Letter C

Step 19. Carefree

Are you learning, laughing, and loving?
I am not trying to get into or out of a relationship.
I am just trying to enjoy the date, Mr. Right Now!

Sharon Esther Lampert

Commitment

Cupid: The Language of Love in Letter C

Step 20. Commitment — Until Death Do Us Part!

Q. Is he here for a reason, a season, or a lifetime?
Q. Is his heart, mind, and penis moving in the same direction?
Q. Is he a soft place to fall when life throws you a curveball?
Q. Are joys doubled & sorrows halved? If so, he is a keeper.
Q. Is he first a best friend before a lover, husband, and father?
Q. Is he a man of character or a charlatan, conman, creep or cheat?

Ask couples who grew old together the secret to their longevity, and they answer the classic question with a similar confession about getting lucky in lust & love, **"I married my best friend!"**
In the words of Supreme Court Justice Ruth Bader Ginsburg, **"It helps to be a little deaf!"**

Happily Married Couples Married Their Best Friends!

Sharon Esther Lampert

Celebration

Cupid: The Language of Love in Letter C

Step 21. Celebration — I Do!

Everything has a lifespan and an expiration date. The loss of
TRUE LOVE is excruciating, and time does not heal a broken heart.
In an **INSANE** world, your **CRAZY** and his **CRAZY** have to align.
Why can't you remember the date of our wedding anniversary!
Q. ADHD? Alzheimer's disease? Early onset of dementia?
All that matters in life is who you love — and who loves you!
Celebrate each day, as if it were your last!

Sharon Esther Lampert

Consummation

Cupid: The Language of Love in Letter C

Step 22. Consummation: Children or Creativity

I am a creative genius. I am a V.E.S.S.E.L. in need of a more than a mere mortal man, but a — MUSE — who will set my extra body part, my "Creative Apparatus" on fire!
I am a test of a man's virility!
Touch me — and live forever in my poem.
Immortality is mine & yours!
Consummation is a creative act — children are birthed — a pyrrhic victory — dust to dust!
Creativity set on fire by one kiss birthed this poem that will live on into perpetuity.

Happy Birthday C.

V.E.S.S.E.L. Very. Extra. Special. Sharon. Esther. Lampert.

Notes:
- This original poem was written on May 9, 2011.
- C. is a real person.
- We did go on a date to celebrate his birthday.
- We went on two dates: May 5th and May 9th, 2011.
- I wrote this poem after he kissed me, and set my "Creative Apparatus" on fire!
- Each year, I added more C words to the poem: 2011-2022.
- The original poem is also in my poetry book, "I Stole All The Words from The Dictionary."

Sharon Esther Lampert

Original Poem: May 9, 2011

CUPID: The Mating Season

Step 1. Connection
On the last cold rainy day of winter,
lingering on into the month of May,
we meet in the middle of a street.
He knows my first name, but not my last
and we can't remember how we met.
Every creature on earth is meeting,
greeting, and preening. Mother nature
is the matchmaker, the yenta busybody
who has set the trap. I am cold, in need of a
sweater and a warm heart and hand to hold.
I am both vulnerable and vixen, a vessel
Ready to be boarded by a seafaring sailor.

Step 2. Chemistry
We stop and stare.
He is tall and handsome.
He is warm and inviting.
We have dinner at Tiny Thai.
I warm up on hot sake and Tom Kha Gai soup.
We celebrate his belated birthday.
We stop at Starbucks for decaffeinated tea,
and share a Chocolate brownie and kisses.
His heart is open and his arms are strong.
Unlike Cinderella, at the stroke of midnight
I am lost in his embrace, drinking his sweet
Elixir of kisses. Two hearts are set aflame.

Step 3. Communication
We talk about this, that, and the other.
It is impossible to know another person.
How was your day?
We take another trip to Peruvian Pio Pio for a
belated (May 9th) Cinco de Mayo celebration
(May 5th). We have become world travelers.
At this juncture in time, I at least know
who I am. We celebrate his good fortune.
We explore Six Handles, the most popular
frozen yogurt joint of sweet Confections.
We share dessert to maintain our figures.
He likes hard ice cream. His favorite is Rocky Road.
We are full but a hunger for love lingers.
We share a non-caloric kiss, and then another.
The world disappears into the background.
Neighbors feel the love emanating from our
embrace and shout out,"It's true love."
His hand has taken hold of my magnificent breast.
The passion between us is spreading
like a raging wildfire, uncontainable.

Step 4. Common Ground
We love learning new things.
He is signed up for a non-credit course.
My mind is a private university where
he can enroll and take a class.

Step 5. Comfortable
He is like a plush teddy bear on the outside.
but on the interior insecurities are percolating.
Demons dance to defeat. He is still single,
in search of a sacred sanctuary built for two.
I am a "special-needs child." My gifts are my glory

Cupid: The Language of Love in Letter C

Step 6. **Compatibility**
I am Leo the lioness. He is Taurus the bull.
We are both fixed organizers (stubborn).
I am positive masculine. I am the Sun.
He is negative feminine. He is Venus.
I am fire, adding LIGHT, making things grow.
He is earth: tactile, stable, sensual, and erotic.
I am a QUEEN. We are both the boss and bossy.
We are destined for a collision, a battle of wills
in the boardroom, not the bedroom.
Opposites don't attract, they attack.

Step 7. **Companionship**
Date, one-night stand, lover, friend, playmate,
Boyfriend, or husband? I enjoy dating and
Having a playmate who loves N.Y.C. nightlife.
Broadway, ballet, museums, sports, and travel.

Step 8. **Collaboration**
Can we work together sharing responsibilities of
raising a family? Or building a home or a business?

Step 9. **Change**
Can he grow, ripen, and mature? Or is
he set in his ways, a dinosaur on the verge
of extinction?

Step 10. **Control** Can we share control?

Step 11. **Conflict** Can we negotiate a resolution?
Change him! Control her! Clash! Crash & Burn!

Step 12. **Conditional**
Adult love is 100% conditional.
Most people don't love you; they love only what they
want from you. Unconditional love is real and rare.
You don't find love, you create love!

Step 13. **Compromise**
"All people help you with their
strengths and hurt you with their
weaknesses." There are no
exceptions to this rule!

Step 14. **Culture of Casual Sex**
Generation Sexual Gratification:
"Sex First. Love Maybe. Marriage
Never."

Step 15. **Carefree**
I am not trying to get into
or out of a relationship.
I am just trying to enjoy the date,
Mr. Right Now.

Step 16. **Commitment**
Is he here for a reason, a season,
or a lifetime?

Step 17. **Celebrate**
Everything has a lifespan and an
expiration date. I love to celebrate
each day, as if it were my last.

Step 18. **Consummation & Creativity**
I am a creative genius in need of
a **MUSE** who can set my extra-body
part, my "Creative Apparatus" on
fire, "I am a test of a man's virility!"
Touch me and live forever in my
poem. Immortality Is Mine & Yours.

Happy Birthday C.!

Sharon Esther Lampert

True Love

True Love is Unconditional.
True Love is Found in the Deed.
True Love is Found in the We.
True Love Unites the Mind,
Body, and Heart as One.

Sharon Esther Lampert

Cupid: The Language of Love in Letter C

How to Read a Poem by Sharon Esther Lampert

1. Sharon's Poetry Paintings
Similar to the poet William Blake, her poems are accompanied by elaborate visual graphics that enrich and compliment the text. The poems are wall hangings, and her poems are framed by ardent fans and hang in their living spaces, like paintings. Students, the world over, read her poems in their classrooms, and use her poetry for their school assignments.

2. Sharon is a Master of Condensation
Sharon is a master of the art of condensation. She is able to condense a major world event in world history into a one-page poem. Her immortal literary gems come in a variety of lengths: A single sentence, a single page, and grand sweeping epics.

3. Sharon is a Literary Photographer
Her poems are telescopic of the main event and microscopic of the infinite details.

4. Sharon Can Pack a Single Verse
Sharon's poems are known for her ability to weave poetry, philosophy, and comedy into a single verse.

5. Documentary Poet: Poems are Cinematic Journey's Through History
Sharon's poems take you on a cinematic journey, and make you feel as if you are reliving the event, as if it happened today.

6. Sharon's Poems are Completed Literary Works
Many poets leave abandoned poems that went unfinished. Sharon's poems are completed works of art. Every word is essential to the poem. You cannot remove or replace a word. There are no extra words. Every word has its rightful place and fits to perfection.

7. Sharon's Poems are All Inspired Works of Art
All of her poems are inspired. There are no rough drafts. Like giving birth to a baby, the poem incubates in her extra-body part a "Creative Apparatus" and is birthed in minutes. Like a baby, the poems are delivered whole and complete.

8. Sharon's Signature Endings: The Epiphany (Spiritual Illumination)
"The Sole Intention of My Poetry Is to Add **LIGHT** to Your Soul" The last verse of every poem delivers a message that educates, enlightens, and empowers. Her searing signature endings find their way into your heart, open your mind to a deeper understanding, and stay with you forever.

Sharon Esther Lampert

- **P**oet
- **P**hilosopher
- **P**eacemaker
- **P**rophet
- **P**erformer: Vocalist
- **P**layer: Jock
- **P**aladin of Education
- **P**HOTON SUPERHERO
- **P**rincess KADIMAH
- **P**rincess & **P**ea
- **P**resident
- **P**ublisher
- **P**roducer
- **P**sychobiologist: Rockefeller U.
- **P**iano-**P**laying Cat
- **P**hoenix
- **P**rodigy
- **P**INUP

NYU
Honored Sharon Lampert with an Award for *Multi-Interdisciplinary Studies* (YOUTUBE video)

24 Websites:
SharonEstherLampert.com
VeryExtraSpecial.com
PhilosopherQueen.com
WorldFamousPoems.com
PoetryJewels.com
PoetryEssentialService.com
GodofWhat.com
Schmaltzy.com
10Miracles.com
TrueLoveBurnsEternal.com
SillyLittleBoys.com
EDUCATION: Smartgrades.com
EDUCATION: EveryDayanEasyA.com
EDUCATION: PhotonSuperHero.com
EDUCATION: BooksNotBombs.com
PlannerParExcellence.com
FloridaRetirementPlanner.com
PalmBeachBookPublisher.com
WritersRunTheWorld.com
Gift Shop: BooksArePowerful.com
Gift Shop: ArtHeart.store
Gift Shop: WorldPeaceEquation.com
Gift Shop: GodIsGoDo.com
Gift Shop: HappyGrandparenting.com

Cupid: The Language of Love in Letter C

About the Prodigy

Sharon Esther Lampert

Gifted: Born with an Extra Body Part, a "Creative Apparatus"

PRODIGY
Unleash the Creator The God Within : 10 Esoteric Laws of Genius and Creativity

POET — One of the World's Greatest Poets
POETRY WORLD RECORD: 120 WORDS OF RHYME
THE GREATEST POEMS EVER WRITTEN ON EXTRAORDINARY WORLD EVENTS
http://famouspoetsandpoems.com/poets.html

PROPHET
22 COMMANDMENTS: All You Will Ever Need to Know About **God**
GOD TALKS TO ME: A Working Definition of God— **GOD IS GO! DO!**

PHILOSOPHER QUEEN
GOD OF WHAT? Is Life a Gift or a Punishment? 10 Absolute Truths
The Sperm Manifesto: 10 Rules for the Road
www.PhilosopherQueen.com

PEACEMAKER
WORLD PEACE EQUATION.com

PALADIN OF EDUCATION
SMARTGRADES BRAIN POWER REVOLUTION
- The Silent Crisis Destroying America's Brightest Minds - "ALMA PUBLIC LIBRARY BOOK OF THE MONTH"
- EVERYDAY AN EASY A!

PHOTON SUPERHERO
SUPERHERO OF EDUCATION
www.PhotonSuperHero.com

PRINCESS & PEA!
- SILLY LITTLE BOYS: 40 Rules of Manhood, www.SillyLittleBoys.com

Sharon BIG BRAIN Conceptualizes BIG IDEAS Using One Letter of the Alphabet:
- TEMPORARY INSANITY: We Are Building Our Lives on a Sand Trap — Written in Letter S
- CUPID: Language of Love — Written in Letter C
- The Secret Sauce of Book Sales — Written in Letter P
- DESTINY: Are You Living Your Life by Default or by Design? — Letter D

PRINCESS KADIMAH
8TH PROPHETESS OF ISRAEL: THE 22 COMMANDMENTS

PIN-UP
SEXIEST CREATIVE GENIUS IN HUMAN HISTORY

Sharon Esther Lampert

THANK YOU
Count Your Blessings. Practice Gratitude.

Blessing 1. My Genetic Gift of Genius—Lefty
- Genetic Inheritance: Painter Maternal Grandfather Benjamin Paikoff & Sculptor Father Abraham Lampert
- Vocalist: Estelle Leibling, Chaim Frieberg, Ashira Orchestra, 18 Years: Ramaz Women's Service (YouTube)
- Athlete: "Faster Than Any Boy, Anytime, Anywhere, Any Age!"

Blessing 2. My Life: The Dawn of the Digital Revolution
- APPLE: The Golden Age of Personal Computers
- ADOBE: The Golden Age of Creativity
- INGRAM: The Golden Age of Publishing
- SOCIAL MEDIA: The Golden Age of the Internet & Global Communication
- iTUNES: The Golden Age of Music & Lyrics
- WIX: The Golden Age of Websites

NYU Professor Laurin Raiken and Me

Blessing 3. My Loved Ones
- Self-Love: Mindfulness, Meditation, and Music Mitigates MADNESS!
- Unconditional Love: Mommy Eve Paikoff Ifcher Lampert
- My PURRfect Children: SCHMALTZY and FALAFEL (Schmaltzy.com)
- My Metaphysical Sister: Poet Hannah Sezenes: "ELI, ELI"
- 7 Practice Husbands, Artist-Muses, Dates and NYC Night Life
- My Bubbe Esther Tulkoff (EstherTulkoff.com)

NYU Professor Karl Bardosh and Me

Blessing 4. My Education, Educators and Awards
My NYU Education: BA, MA, MA, and Awards: (YOUTUBE videos)
- NYU Professor Laurin Raiken
  NYU "Multi-Interdisciplinary Award" and M.A. Class Representative at Graduation
- NYC Rockefeller University, Publication: "Hyperphagia and Obesity Induced by Neuropeptide Y" — Lab of Dr. Sarah Leibowitz and Dr. Glen Stanley
- 100-Year Scholarship Award Winner, Presented by NYC Mayor Edward Koch
- Empire Science Scholarship Award Winner
- Jerusalem Fellowship Award, Aish Hatorah, Israel
- First Prize: Upper East Side Resident Writing Contest

NYU President Jay Oliva and Me Class Representative at my Graduation

Blessing 5. My Sports
- NYC Marathon
- Basketball: NYU Women's Varsity Basketball Team, Center
- Basketball: NYC Urban Professional League
- Skiing: Heavenly, Lake Tahoe, Nevada
- Tennis: NYC Central Park Tennis Courts
- NYU Weightlifting Contest Winner! NYU Coles Sports Center
 (I was the only contestant-so I won!)

NYU President Andrew Hamilton and Me

Blessing 6. My Inspirations
- ISRAEL: "AM YISRAEL CHAI!" (Lambs to Slaughter to LIONS and Light of the World!)
- NYC: The Golden Age of Personal Freedom & Self-Expression

Cupid: The Language of Love in Letter C

Artists March to the Beat of a Different Drummer
Sharon Esther Lampert Marches to the Beats of an Entire Orchestra

**Poet, Philosopher, Prophet, Peacemaker
Paladin of Education, Princess & Pea
Phoenix, PHOTON, PINUP, Prodigy**

Blue-Eyed. Brilliant. Beautiful. Buxom. Books. Blessed.

Sharon Esther Lampert was born an OLD SOUL—She was never young! Sharon is a lefty.

At age nine, her mother declared: "My daughter is a poet, philosopher, and teacher!" She nicknamed her daughter, "The Princess and the Pea!"

Sharon's greatest literary works woke her up in the middle of the night—and made her get up out of bed—and write them down. Sharon writes an entire book in one day!

Sharon's mother was the sole person in Sharon's life who knew who she was from the INSIDE OUT—and what would become of her. Her beloved mother also knew to her very last breath… the exact day and to the minute when she would die! (Eve Paikoff Lampert: June 3, 1925—May 5, 1985).

Sharon Esther's Gifts are Metaphysical—Beyond the Scope of Scientific Inquiry

There Are No Rough Drafts!—The Books Write Themselves!
(There Are 4 Books with God in the Title)

"A LIST" Sharon Esther Lampert is One of the World's Greatest Poets
http://famouspoetsandpoems.com/poets.html

#1 Poetry Website for School Projects

On a global scale, Sharon's poetry is used by teachers for their poetry lesson plans, and by students for their poetry projects.

New York University Awards—(YOUTUBE videos)

Sharon Esther earned three degrees from NYU—and she was honored with two NYU awards. Sharon represented her class at her graduation—and was honored with an award for "Multi-Interdisciplinary Studies." She also played on the NYU Women's Varsity Basketball Team as a center in the $16 million Coles Sports Center. Sharon won an "NYU Weightlifting Contest"—Sharon was the sole contestant—so she won! (NYU newspaper article).

Sharon Esther Lampert

FAN MAIL

FANS@SharonEstherLampert.com
(FAN MAIL will be published in Sharon's books)

Ardent Fan Harry McVeety

A PHENOMENON...
SHARON ESTHER LAMPERT

Lithe and lovely ... like a fawn.
This lady fascinates me ... from dusk till dawn.
Feminine and comely ... she's beyond belief
A blue-beam from her eyes ... is my soothing relief.

Girlish in her braces ... maidenly in her style
I yearn for her embraces ... and adore her friendly smile.
As tasteful as any artist ... you'll ever see
She's a compendium of class ... from A to Z.

If you'd like to see a figure, that puts Venus to shame
Behold her in a swimsuit, and your passions will aflame.
Ever exuding goodness . . . guided from above
Miss Sharon is the essence, and epitome of Love.

She's the inspiration of sages, and also fools like me
And the most magnificent female, I'm sure I'll ever see.
The nights are now endearing, & never filled with doubt
I sometimes wake up singing, cause it's Sharon . . .
I dream about.

Affectionately, . .
A devoted fan,
—Harry McVeety

Cupid: The Language of Love in Letter C

FAN MAIL

FANS@SharonEstherLampert.com

(FAN MAIL will be published in Sharon's books)

Ardent Fan Cody Howell, H.S. Student

Cody Howell
1042 Prospect Dr.
Imperial, Mo 63052
May 2, 2005

Sharon Esther Lampert
P.O.BOX 103,
New York, New York, 10028, US

Dear, Sharon E. Lampert

Hello, My name is Cody, I am a Junior at Windsor High School in Missouri. I have had the chance to write to any one person and I picked you. I have always enjoyed quotes and sayings. Theirs just something about it, like I have always known there is a "better way" but never really found anything until I started to pay attention that their was more than just physical happenings. The poet has the ability to drink from streams science has yet to discover. I used to always reads one liners like
" a community begins to grow when old men plant trees they know they will never enjoy the shade of." Things like this really interested me. Something more than what I had known.

I am very curious by nature, and this kind of wisdom/intellect really hit the spot for me, now I have many poems, sayings, quotes ext. I can't recite them by heart but I thourouly enjoyed the ones I read. I didn't know of you until me and my buddy were talking about how we like psychology and basically more than average and the "better way". After reading some of your quotes I realized you must have seen your share of happenings and become very wise over the years of thought, poetry, and life.

My first thought was to write to you and try to flatter you because I enjoyed your work. Well I guess you made your poetry your work. Then I started thinking that this well of knowledge , all that stuff you've learned, it would be a long shot but my curiosity wouldn't stop unless if I asked you if you could share some of the knowledge you have gained. Any and all would be appreciated and probably useful later considering I am still just a 17-year-old kid. I can't think of any other word than greedy, but you have already thought so many with your influences, and I ask you to help me out, If your busy you have already done more than enough, thank you, and thanks for your time while reading this. I am sorry but I always find myself looking for more and I'm positive you have gained useful info in your day. I could imagine the child who has heard many stories, lesions, and wisdoms of many. He'd be one of the most diverse ,intelligent humans around, and with something like this in mind how could I not be greedy.

I have already learned some from Internet, friends like the one who told me about poems, and family. I have tried to learn patience from the impatient, kindness from the angry, and truth from fools, but for some reason I'm not thankful for these teachers. I still feel as if I could have more, and the lessons of an older experienced poet just has something about how it sounds. Greatness is all I've seen come from poets their ability to make one think is amazing , I could just imagine the wisdom of an experienced one.

Either way I just wanted to say thank you for your time and thank you for doing what you have done. Your shared wisdom and lessons will help many and your work might not be remembered forever but I believe that your positive effect will. Thank you again

Your student ,
Cody

Sharon Esther Lampert

Kadimah Press: Gifts of Genius

Revelation! — My Books Write Themselves!

Poet: The Greatest Poems Ever Written on Extraordinary World Events
Title: I Stole All the Words from the Dictionary
ISBN Hardcover: 978-1-885872-06-7
ISBN Paperback: 978-1-885872-07-4
ISBN E-Book: 978-1-885872-08-1

18 Books of Poetry

Prophet: WORLD PREMIERE!
Title: GOD TALKS TO ME: A Working Definition of God
ISBN Hardcover: 978-1-885872-33-3
ISBN Paperback: 978-1-885872-34-0
ISBN E-Book: 978-1-885872-36-4

Prophet: WORLD PREMIERE!
A Universal Moral Compass For All Religions, For All People, For All Time
Title: The 22 Commandments: All You Will Ever Need to know About GOD
ISBN Hardcover: 978-1-885872-03-6
ISBN Paperback: 978-1-885872-04-3
ISBN E-Book: 978-1-885872-05-0

Philosopher: WORLD PREMIERE!
Title: God of What? Is Life a Gift or a Punishment?
ISBN Hardcover: 978-1-885872-00-5
ISBN Paperback: 978-1-885872-01-2
ISBN E-Book: 978-1-885872-02-9
Website: GodofWhat.com

No Fakes!
No Fat!
No Fluff!
No Filler!
No Flops!
No F-Bomb!

Prodigy: WORLD PREMIERE!
Title: Unleash the Creator The God Within: 10 Esoteric Laws of Genius and Creativity
ISBN Hardcover: 978-1-885872-21-0
ISBN Paperback: 978-1-885872-22-7
ISBN E-Book: 978-1-885872-23-4

Cupid: The Language of Love in Letter C

Kadimah Press: Gifts of Genius

Prodigy: WORLD PREMIERE!
Title: CUPID: The Language of Love — Written in Letter C
ISBN Hardcover: 978-1-885872-55-5
ISBN Paperback: 978-1-885872-56-2
ISBN E-Book: 978-1-885872-57-9
Website: SharonEstherLampert.com

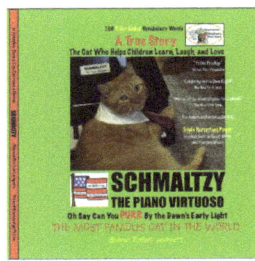

Popular: Children's Book — True Story of a Piano-Playing Cat
Title: SCHMALTZY: In America, Even a Cat Can Have a Dream
ISBN Hardcover: 978-1-885872-39-5
ISBN Paperback: 978-1-885872-38-8
ISBN E-Book: 978-1-885872-37-1
Website: Schmaltzy.com

Color-Coded Vocabulary Words Before Every Chapter

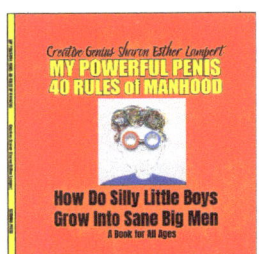

Popular: WORLD PREMIERE!
Title: SILLY LITTLE BOYS: 40 RULES OF MANHOOD
How Do Silly Little Boys Grow into Big Sane Men?
For Men of All Ages — 14 Global Catastrophes of Violence Against Women
ISBN Hardcover: 978-1-885872-29-6
ISBN Paperback: 978-1-885872-35-7
ISBN E-Book: 978-1-885872-41-8
Website: SillyLittleBoys.com

Popular: Every Great Relationship Begins with the Perfect Meal
Title: SEX ON A PLATE: FOOD AS FOREPLAY
The Cookbook of Everlasting Love
ISBN Hardcover: 978-1-885872-46-3
ISBN Paperback: 978-1-885872-48-7
ISBN E-Book: 978-1-885872-47-0
Website: TrueLoveBurnsEternal.com

Sharon Esther Lampert

I Am Mortal. My Book Is Immortal.
My Books Are My Remains.
Please Handle Them Gently!

This book was compiled in 4 parts:
Part 1. Birth of Poem — May 9, 2011
Part 2. More C Words — 2011-2022
Part 3. Format Book — May 2022
Part 4. Publish Book — May 24, 2022

Sharon Esther Lampert
SEE THE WORLD THROUGH THE EYES OF A CREATIVE GENIUS
Poet, Philosopher, Prophet, Peacemaker, Princess & Pea, PINUP, Prodigy

FANS@SharonEstherLampert.com

www.ingramcontent.com/pod-product-compliance
Lightning Source LLC
Chambersburg PA
CBHW051318110526
44590CB00031B/4399